The colors of the clouds:

Clouds are not always white. In fact they present a variety of colors: pink, gold, yellow, orange, grey or blue. Their position in the sky, the time of day, and weather conditions all serve to determine their color.

On sunny days the upper part of a cloud appears radiant white, while the shadows are concentrated underneath. This lower area should be colored blue and violet with gentle, superimposed strokes.

Storm clouds are gray and brown. They appear to have more volume, even density, than other clouds, so to draw them it is necessary to create shapes inside them and to leave a white outline around the areas that are shaded in grey.

The colors of clouds are most spectacular when the dusk lights up the sky with orange tones. Then clouds appear to have a rich yellow-orange light that is reflected in their lower part. Violet covers the shaded area.

When a cloud is located in front of the sun a backlighting effect occurs. In this case a cloud's contour appears white while its center takes on a grey-blue color.

Drawing rain

To draw rain add a section of diagonal lines below a cloud to indicate the effect of rain falling on the landscape. The deeper and sharper the strokes, the more intense the rain will appear to be.

W9-BUI-575

FIELD GUIDES

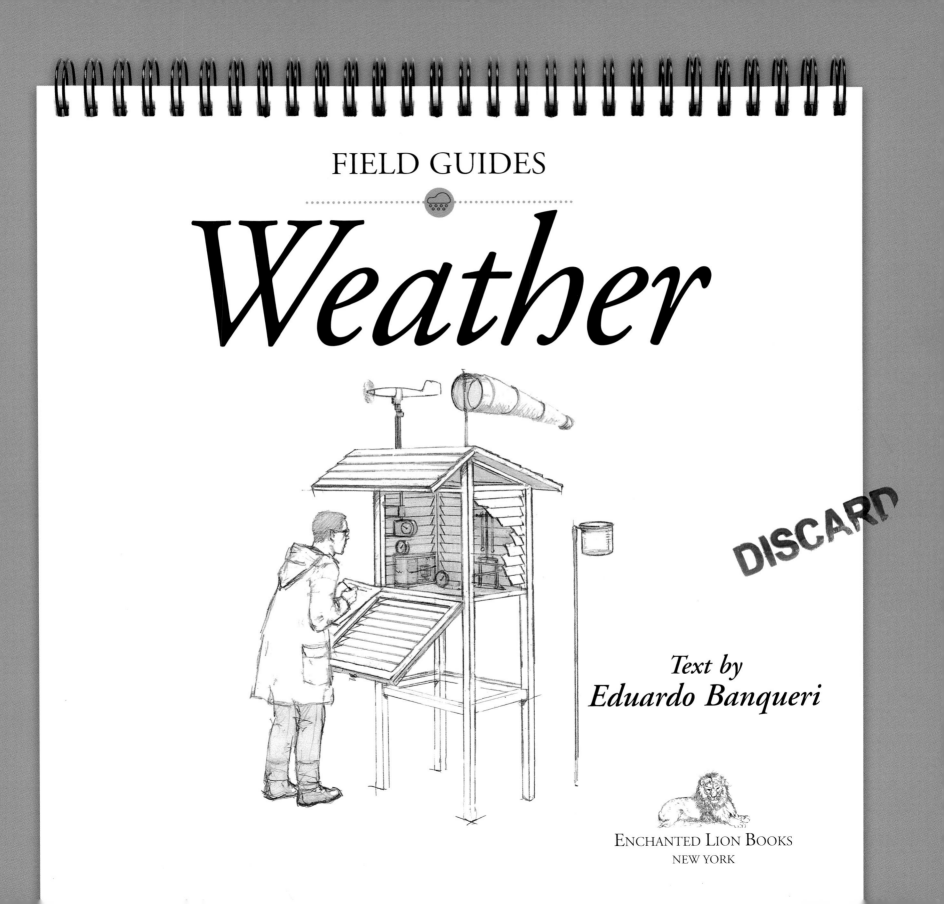

Weather

Text by
Eduardo Banqueri

ENCHANTED LION BOOKS
NEW YORK

First American Edition published in 2006 by
Enchanted Lion Books, 45 Main Street, Suite 519
Brooklyn, NY 11201

© 2005 Parramón Ediciones, S.A
Imprint of Grupo Editorial Norma
Translation © 2006 Parramón Ediciones, S.A.

Conception and realization
Parramón Ediciones, S.A.

Editor
Lluís Borràs

Assistant Editor
Cristina Vilella

Text
Eduardo Banqueri

Graphic design and layout
Estudi Toni Inglès

Photography
AGE-Fotostock, Boreal, Manuel Clemente, Sincronia

Illustrations
Estudio Marcel Socías
Gabi Martin (flyleafs)

Director of Production
Rafael Marfil

Production
Manel Sánchez

For information about permissions to reproduce
selections from this book, write to Permissions,
Enchanted Lion Books, 45 Main Street, Suite 519,
Brooklyn, NY 11201

A CIP record is on file with the Library of Congress

ISBN 1-59270-059-4

Printed in Spain

2 4 6 8 10 9 7 5 3 1

CONTENTS

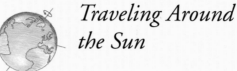
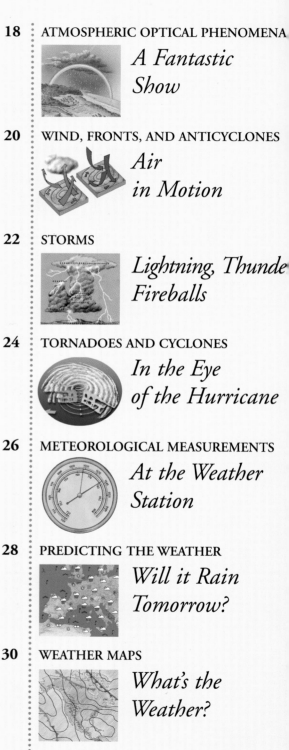

Natural Phenomena

Meteorology is one of the fields of science that has had the greatest influence on human life. From the earliest explanations of atmospheric phenomena as manifestations of the gods to the strictest scientific interpretations of today, the weather has not ceased to be an object of study. Meteorology seeks to comprehend and explain the laws that govern the weather, and thereby to anticipate future phenomena.

Nevertheless, meteorology remains a little known science. Even though most people talk frequently about "the weather," they still have only vague notions about the atmospheric physics that create it.

The objective of this book is to help the reader to understand the natural phenomena that take place in the atmosphere, particularly those that can be observed directly. We hope that by offering explanations and insights into the mysteries of meteorology, this book will motivate the reader to obtain a deeper knowledge of this fascinating field.

Interest in the Weather

Meteorology is the study of the atmosphere and the phenomena that occur in it. The sun provides the necessary energy, and its heat, combined with water and wind, leads to what are called meteorological phenomena: atmospheric pressure, ambient temperature, humidity of the air, air currents, visibility, cloudiness and precipitations.

Is the weather the same as climate?

We often confuse meteorology with climatology, even though they are two different concepts. Climate is the average whole of meteorological phenomena that are characteristic of a given region and are repeated cyclically. On the other hand, weather is the whole of meteorological phenomena in a specific place at a specific time.

We use the weather to describe the daily variations in temperature, humidity, cloudiness, wind and precipitations that take place in the air (atmosphere) right around us.

The meteorological conditions maintained over thousands of years determine the characteristics of a landscape as well as its climate. For example, desert sand is a product of the abrupt changes in temperature that occur in the desert between day and night. Those changes, together with the buffeting action of the wind, serve to break down rock into sand. The wind also works to transport the sand, forming it into dunes.

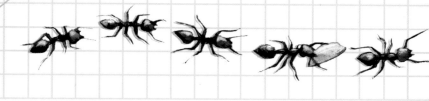

Why does the weather change?

The sun is the source of all of the changes that occur in the atmosphere. Due to the inclination of the Earth with respect to the sun, the equatorial zones receive more intense radiations than do the poles. Moreover, due to the movement of the Earth in orbit, its position in relation to the sun varies in the course of the year, causing meteorological conditions to change as well, which is why there are seasons.

Life adapts to weather cycles

Plants and animals have developed strategies that make it possible for them to survive and adapt themselves to seasonal changes. Plants flower in the spring, leaves fall in the autumn, ants work in the summer, and rest in the winter, bears hibernate, and so on.

Migratory birds travel thousands of miles every year to escape from the cold of winter and the high heat of summer.

Traveling Around the Sun

The effects of the sun and the movement of the Earth in relation to it are the principal causes of meteorological and climatic variations. Our planet has two main astronomic movements: in rotation and in orbit. These movements bring about the alternation of day and night, the change of seasons, and the resulting differences in temperature between different points on our planet, thereby causing all of the meteorological phenomena that we know.

movement in rotation

The earth's distance from the sun changes

Since the Earth's orbit around the sun is elliptical, the distance between the two varies depending on the time of year. Our planet is closest to the sun at the beginning of January (perihelion), closer than at the beginning of July (aphelion), which means that it receives more heat in the first month of the year than in the middle of the year. For this reason, along with other factors such as the angle of the sun, winter in the northern hemisphere is not as cold as in the southern and summer in the southern hemisphere is hotter than in the northern.

→ at the poles the sun's rays fall obliquely, so less energy reaches them than there would at a different angle

→ in the tropics the energy that comes from the sun is greater due to the fact that the sun's rays fall on the earth's surface almost perpendicularly

→ in the temperate zones of the Earth the angle of the sun's rays changes depending on the season of the year. In summer the rays are perpendicular to the surface and there are more hours of sunlight than in winter

→ the Earth's axis is tilted 23.5 degrees. The the Earth's orbit around the sun rotates the area of the planet that is tilted toward the star, so the intensity of the heat that reaches the Earth varies depending on the time of year

summer   winter

winter   summer

When the northern hemisphere is tilted toward the sun then it is summer on that part of the Earth since the sun's rays fall more perpendicularly. Meanwhile, in the southern hemisphere the rays fall obliquely and for that reason it is winter. Summer in the southern hemisphere takes place when the northern hemisphere is tilted away from the sun.

The four seasons do not have the same duration

This is due to the fact that the Earth makes its journey with a speed that is variable, going faster the closer it is to the sun and slower the further away it is. Thus the extremes of each season are not the same for the two hemispheres.

movement
in orbit

Spring

By winter's end the sun has moved higher in the sky and the days are getting longer. Nights are cold, but the days are warm. In the northern hemisphere, spring begins on the 20th or 21st of March. This is when cold weather begins to wane, trees, plants and meadows begin to get green again, flowers begin to bloom, and it starts to get warm.

Summer

Summer begins in the northern hemisphere on the 20th or 21st of June. The sun is very high in the sky and days are long and hot. This is the hottest season, and from time to time there are storms.

Fall

This is the season when the leaves fall from the trees and the weather begins to cool off. In the northern hemisphere fall begins on the 21st or 22nd of September. Nights grow longer and colder and in the morning there is often fog and sometimes frost.

Winter

This is the coldest season of the year. The days are shorter than the nights, and the sun is so low that it almost fails to warm the earth. In the northern hemisphere winter begins on the 21st or 22nd of December.

A Mosaic of Climates

Due to the curve of the Earth and the 23.5° inclination of its axis of rotation, insulation varies from the equator to the poles, causing important differences in weather conditions, which, in turn, have shaped the climate and landscape of each area of our planet. The tropics and the polar circles mark the division of the Earth into five astronomical zones that contain seven different climatic zones: an equatorial zone, two tropical zones, two temperate zones and two polar zones.

For any given area of the Earth we need to consider not just its latitude (which determines the inclination of the sun and thus the amount of the sun's warmth that reaches the surface of the Earth), but also its altitude, the characteristics of the area, its distance from the ocean, the type of currents present, and its location in relation to mountain or lake systems.

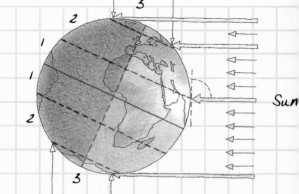

Sun

1. The intertropical or low latitude zone that goes from the equator (0°) to the tropics (23° 27'). The temperature is relatively high all year round because the sun's rays fall vertically.

2. The temperate or middle latitude zones that go from the tropics (23° 27') to the polar circles (66° 33'). The sun's rays are more inclined or oblique, so there are great differences in temperature and in the duration of day and night between the seasons.

3. The polar or high latitude zones that go from the polar circles (66° 33') to the parallel 90°. Since the rays fall tangentially or almost parallel to the surface, it is cold throughout all the months of the year.

Although the crater of Kilimanjaro is only several hundred miles from the equator, it is perpetually covered with snow on account of its altitude.

Equatorial zone

This is situated around the equator. Temperatures are high and consistent, with very little variation. The rains, which are very intense, are often seasonal but continue during a great part of the year. All this favors the growth of vegetation, and it is here that we find the great rainforests.

Seasonal tropical zones

These are located to the north and to the south of the equatorial zone. There are no cold seasons though there are one or two rainy seasons with one or two dry seasons between them.

Despite being close to the Arctic Circle, Reykjavik has a moderate climate thanks to the ocean's currents.

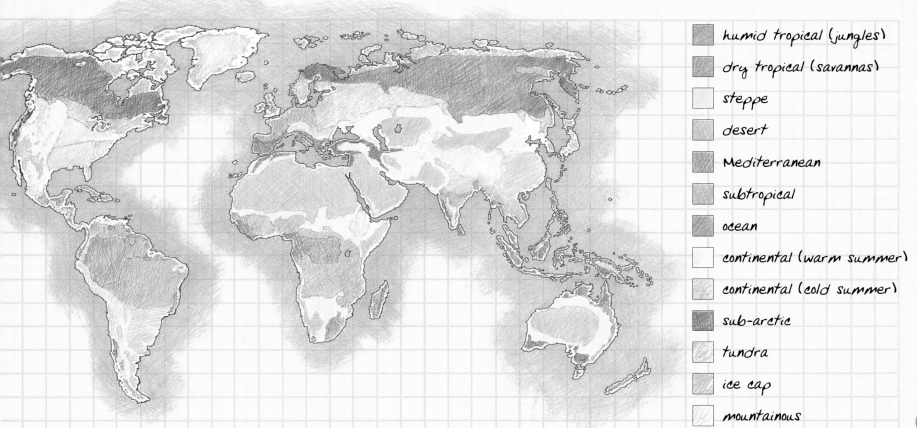

humid tropical (jungles)

dry tropical (savannas)

steppe

desert

Mediterranean

subtropical

ocean

continental (warm summer)

continental (cold summer)

sub-arctic

tundra

ice cap

mountainous

Desert tropical zones

In these zones evaporation is greater than precipitation, which normally does not go over 10 inches of rain per year. There also is a good chance that it may not rain at all. The fluctuations in temperature between day and night are significant (up to 40° difference).

Temperate zones with a Mediterranean climate

These are coastal zones located between the subtropical and humid temperate zones. Winters are gentle and damp with a highly irregular distribution of rain (more plentiful in spring and fall) and dry, sunny summers.

Humid temperate zones

These are located to the north (northern hemisphere) or south (southern hemisphere) of the tropical zones. Summers are mild and damp and winters are cold with frequent snowfalls. Annual precipitation ranges between 20-60 inches of rain.

Sub-arctic zones

These are zones of transition between the temperate zones and the arctic or polar areas. Winters are long and severe. There is no real summer. The sparse precipitation (about 12 inches per year) is almost always in the form of snow. Average temperatures range between 5-40°F.

Arctic zones

These have low temperatures all year round that can reach extreme levels in the long polar nights. Precipitation is very sparse (less than 10 inches per year) and always in the form of snow or ice. Temperatures rise to above 32° F during only two or three months of the year. Strong winds blow almost all year long and serve to dry the air even more.

A Highly Active Mixture of Gases

What we call the atmosphere is the layer of gases that surrounds the Earth and is maintained in position by the force of gravitational attraction. It is made up chiefly of nitrogen (78%) and oxygen (21%). Although other gases, such as carbon dioxide (CO_2), and water vapor are present in far smaller amounts, they still are of crucial importance from a meteorological point of view. The components of the atmosphere are found concentrated close to the surface of the Earth, compacted by the force of gravity. As altitude increases, the density of the atmosphere decreases very rapidly.

The weight of the air or atmospheric pressure

This rapidly diminishes as we go up. There also are differences in pressure between different zones of the troposphere that are of great interest for climatology. This is because air moves from high pressure areas to those of lower pressure, which is how winds are formed.

A highly irregular distribution of gases

Half the total mass of atmospheric matter can be found quite close to the Earth, in an area that extends 3 1/2 miles up from sea level. Indeed, 95% of this matter can be found within a mere 9 miles of altitude up from the Earth.

exosphere

thermopause

thermosphere

mesopause

mesosphere

stratopause

stratosphere

tropopause
troposphere

troposphere– the densest layer of the atmosphere. Meteorological phenomena (rain, wind, changes in temperature, etc.) take place here, and its composition makes the development of life possible. It extends from sea level to about 5 miles above the surface of the Earth at the poles and 10 miles at the equator. In the troposphere the temperature goes down as it gets higher, reaching -94°F at its upper limit.

tropopause–the boundary between the troposphere and the stratosphere.

stratosphere–the layer that begins at the tropopause, and reaches an upper limit called the stratopause at an altitude of 30 miles up. At this level the temperature changes direction and rises from -94° F to around 32°F in the stratopause. There is almost no vertical movement of the air, but horizontal winds frequently reach 125 miles/h. From 18-32 miles up, we find the ozone layer, which plays a critical role in the absorption of harmful ultraviolet radiations from the sun.

stratopause–the boundary between the stratosphere and the mesosphere.

mesosphere–in this layer temperature again descends as altitude increases, reaching -130° F. Here the density of the air is very low, though it maintains the same proportion of components as in the troposphere. Meteorites are destroyed when they hit this layer of the atmosphere.

mesopause–the boundary between the mesosphere and the thermosphere.

thermosphere–here the density of the air is very low and the few atoms it contains are ionized, so this zone is also called the ionosphere. Here the aurora borealis occurs, and it is here that artificial satellites orbit the Earth. Temperature is so high that it can reach 2,696° F.

thermopause–the boundary between the thermosphere and the exosphere

exosphere–here there is a great variety of gases such as helium, nitrogen, oxygen and argon, but in very small quantities, since the lack of gravity at this altitude makes it possible for molecules to easily escape into space. Temperatures range from 572°F – 3,002°F.

11

All About Atmospheric Conditions

Meteorological factors correspond to the variables that we must take into account when determining atmospheric conditions in order to be able to predict the weather. The key factors, or parameters, are: pressure, temperature, humidity, wind, cloud cover and precipitation.

What we have to put up with

The total weight of the atmosphere is about 6,000 billion tons. However, we hardly notice this weight. At sea level the body is subject to a peripheral pressure of a bit more than 2 1/2 pounds/cm, but that pressure on the skin is balanced by the outward pressure of the air coming into the lungs and blood. For this reason we do not notice the approximately 40,000 pounds of pressure that each of us withstands.

atmospheric pressure

This is the weight of the atmosphere on a specific point of the Earth's surface. Measurement is done with a barometer and can be expressed in different units of measure, either hectopascals (hPa) (formerly called millibars (mbar)) or millimeters of mercury (mm Hg). Average pressure at sea level is 1013 hPa or 760 mm Hg.

air temperature

On a global scale temperatures are distributed according to latitude, though solar radiation is not the only parameter that is involved. The amount of water vapor and carbon dioxide (CO_2) present also affect temperature, as do atmospheric density and pressure.

humidity in the air

There is always a certain amount of water vapor in the atmosphere, which varies from one place to another and one moment to another. The quantity of vapor depends on air temperature. The warmer it is, the more water vapor the air can retain.

The greater the difference in temperature and pressure between two areas, the stronger the wind.

Cloud cover is the extension of sky covered by clouds and is expressed in eighths of sky covered, or octas.

Symbol	octas	Sky	Symbol	octas	Sky
○	0/8	Clear	◓		Cloudy
◍	1/8	Partly cloudy	◕	6/8	Mostly cloudy
◔	2/8	Partly cloudy	◕	7/8	Mostly cloudy
◔	3/8	Partly cloudy	●	8/8	Overcast
◑	4/8	Cloudy			

13

cloud coverage

When humidity reaches 100% the air cannot contain any more water in the form of vapor, which therefore begins to condense into microscopic drops of liquid and ice in suspension, floating in the air and forming clouds or fog.

precipitations

In the clouds there are little drops of water that are normally between 8 and 15 micra in diameter, depending on the type of cloud. When these drops grow to over 0.1 mm they fall in the form of precipitation. Thus rain is the fall, or precipitation, of drops of water produced by the condensation of water vapor in the atmosphere.

wind

Wind is air in motion, caused by differences in pressure and temperature between different areas. Wind goes from high pressure to low pressure areas, in an attempt to equalize the pressure. There are two important parameters relating to wind: speed (which indicates whether it is strong or weak) and direction (where it comes from).

When the Sky is Covered

A cloud is a collection of fine water particles in a liquid or solid state (ice crystals) that form masses of variable thickness, color and shape. These particles or drops of water are spherical and very small (between .004 and .1 mm) and are suspended in the air in constant movement, banging into one another and grouping together. When their thickness increases to the point that their weight is greater than that of ascending forces, they fall to the ground.

cirrostratus

cumulonimbus

Clouds of water and clouds of ice

The exterior appearance of a cloud is determined by its composition to a great extent. Thus a cloud of ice will present a smooth, fibrous appearance while a water cloud will have more rounded, cottony outlines.

From water vapor to cloud

Water vapor in the air condenses to form clouds due to a cooling off. When it cools to "dew point" temperature (the temperature at which the air reaches saturation) it no longer can retain all its humidity in the form of vapor, which quickly condenses to drops.

nimbostratus

stratus

altostratus

cirrocumulus

cirrus

altocumulus

stratocumulus

cumulus

Ten types of clouds

Clouds are classified into ten types that are grouped together into four categories according to the altitude at which they are formed: high, medium, low, or vertically developed. These ten types take four general forms: cirrus (filamentous clouds), cumulus (clouds with a fluffy look), stratus (formation in layers) and nimbus (opaque). Cumulous clouds develop vertically, stratus horizontally, and nimbus have a high level of both vertical and horizontal development.

high clouds (cirrus, cirrocumulus and cirrostratus)

These have their bases at an altitude of 16,400 – 26,000 feet and are formed largely of ice crystals. As they have little opacity, they are hard to see during the day, but are visible at dawn and dusk.

medium clouds (altocumulus and altostratus)

With bases at an altitude of 6,500 – 16,400 feet, these are principally made up of drops of water. However, as they can easily reach the borderline with high clouds they also can contain ice crystals. Consequently, they can be either opaque or highly translucent.

low clouds (stratus, stratocumulus and nimbostratus)

These have their bases at an altitude of 985 – 6,500 feet. They are made up of water drops, throw their own shadows and can become highly developed.

Vertically developed clouds (cumulus and cumulonimbus)

These can be found at all levels of the troposphere and even in the stratosphere. They develop as a result of warm air rising from the surface of the earth. Because of the height to which they rise and their stormy effects, these clouds produce some of the most interesting atmospheric phenomena.

Water in the Atmosphere

It used to be that any atmospheric phenomenon other than a cloud, such as a rainbow, lightning, or snow, was called a "meteor." Following from this, the term "hydrometeor" refers specifically to all the possible ways, with the exception of clouds, in which water can be present in the atmosphere: rain, drizzle, sleet, snow, fog, dew and frost. The size of particles ranges from .2 millimeters to centimeters (approximately 1 inch).

Each type of rain has a name

We say it's drizzling when the drops that fall are tiny (with a diameter of less than .5 millimeters) and seem to be sprayed as if floating in the air. We call the drops that are falling "rain" if they're continuous, regular and have a diameter over .5 millimeters. A heavy shower occurs if drops fall suddenly and intensely over a short period of time, or we say it's a downpour if drops fall violently and abundantly enough to provoke flooding.

rain

is the fall or precipitation of drops of water that come from condensation in the atmosphere and have a diameter over .5 millimeters

snow

is the precipitation of ramified or star-shaped ice crystals. On the other hand, balls of ice of a diameter of 5 - 50 millimeters are called hail or hailstones.

sleet

is a type of precipitation in which water is present in two states and forms a mixture of frozen and liquid water.

Types of clouds and precipitations

The different types of hydrometeors are associated with specific kinds of clouds.

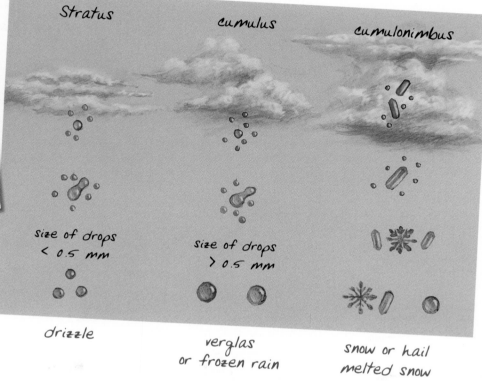

Stratus

cumulus

cumulonimbus

size of drops
< 0.5 mm

size of drops
> 0.5 mm

drizzle

verglas
or frozen rain

snow or hail
melted snow
rain

17

fog

s a suspension of tiny drops of
water close to the ground that
reduces horizontal visibility to
about a 1/2 mile. If visibility
s over a 1/2 mile, it is called
mist.

dew

consists of deposits of
condensed water vapor.

frost

consists of deposits of frozen
water.

A Fantastic Show

The sun's rays must pass through the Earth's atmosphere—with all the phenomena that take place in it and all the particles and molecules the air contains—before reaching the surface of the Earth. On this journey the sun's light undergoes a series of changes that bring about optical phenomena that have intrigued human beings throughout history.

crepuscular rays

These are observed a little after sunset on the western horizon or a little before sunrise in the eastern sky. Crepuscular rays appear as a result of the reflection and diffusion of the sun's rays in the upper levels of the atmosphere before dawn and after dusk. The yellow or white color of the light announces the arrival of clouds.

the blue of the sky

This is due to the fact that particles and drops in the air disperse the shorter wavelengths of sunlight (those found at the blue end of the spectrum) more than the longer wavelengths (located at the red end). The cleaner the air, the darker blue the sky will be.

halo phenomena

A halo is a ring that is either white or a very pale color that sometimes appears around the sun or the moon. It is produced by the refraction and reflection of light on the ice crystals in the atmosphere.

Polar auroras

These are storms of sparks and rays of light that appear to form a curtain over the sky as they fall. In these storms the colors red and violet appear to intertwine and melt into one another. This amazing spectacle, known in regions of the northern hemisphere as the "aurora borealis" and as the "aurora australis" in the southern hemisphere, occurs in the ionosphere and is caused by the shock of electrons from solar emissions colliding with gas molecules from the upper layers of the earth's atmosphere.

Everything in order

The colors of the rainbow are always seen in the same order: red, orange, yellow, green, blue, indigo (dark blue) and violet.

coronas

A circular white or yellow surface can sometimes be observed around the sun and the moon. It is produced by the diffraction of sunlight or moonlight in drops of water that are present in the cloud stratus at medium altitude.

rainbow

For a rainbow, gleaming with all the colors of the spectrum, to appear in one's field of vision, the sun must be located behind the observer and must strike a curtain of rain that is directly in front of the observer. A rainbow appears as a result of the refraction and reflection of the sun's rays on tiny raindrops.

the other colors of the sky

When the sun is low, light passes through particles of atmospheric dust that for the most part disperse the longer wavelengths, causing the sun to take on a red color, which largely happens at dawn and dusk. The little drops of water in clouds and fog diffuse all colors equally, making the sky look white.

Air in Motion

The cause of all atmospheric movement is the unequal heating up of the Earth's surface by the sun. As a result of the differences in temperature that occur, a complex pattern of atmospheric circulation works to transfer heat from warmer regions to the poles in order to compensate for these disparities.

Warm front

When a mass of warm air hits a mass of cold air a warm front is formed. The warm air gradually rises above the layer of cold air, forming clouds that can lead to long rainy periods

With anticyclonic weather there is sunshine and good visibility.

Cold front

Cold air advances toward warm air and goes under it. This causes the warm air to rise, forming clouds that cause hard rains and storms.

Fronts

When two large air masses of different, but uniform temperatures come together, a collision occurs that creates a sudden change in humidity and temperature. The line where the two masses meet is called a "front."

Wind

Wind is the movement of air that is brought about by the differences in temperature that exist due to the unequal warming of different areas of the Earth and the atmosphere. As warmer air masses rise their place is occupied by surrounding, cooler air masses that also are denser. Wind is thus produced by the displacement of air from high pressure areas toward low pressure areas.

Cyclones and anticyclones

rising air
In the northern hemisphere rising air moves counter-clockwise, while in the southern hemisphere it moves clockwise.

descending air
This air moves clockwise in the northern hemisphere, while in the southern hemisphere it moves counter-clockwise.

Air in motion

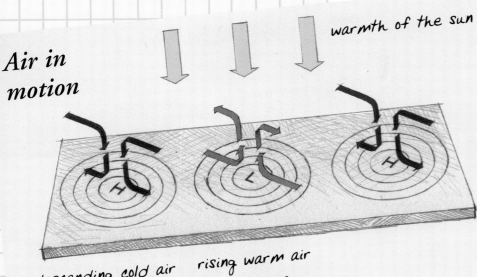

warmth of the sun

descending cold air
high pressure

rising warm air
low pressure

Anticyclone

An anticyclone is a zone where atmospheric pressure is higher than in the surrounding area. As air pressure does not change rapidly in a high pressure area, winds are gentle. As the air mass descends, we have clear skies and dry weather.

Low pressure area (cyclone or depression)

A cyclone is an area of low atmospheric pressure. Characterized by a mass of rising air, it originates strong winds and causes cloudy skies, rain or snow.

Lightning, Thunder, Fireballs

Storms, which can be extremely violent, are one of the most spectacular atmospheric phenomena. They are characterized by the presence of a cumulonimbus cloud, lightning, thunder, strong winds and precipitation in the form of heavy rain or hail.

first phase of development
The warming of the Earth's surface creates a rising air current that gradually cools down until it is condensed enough to form a cumulus cloud.

The formation of a storm

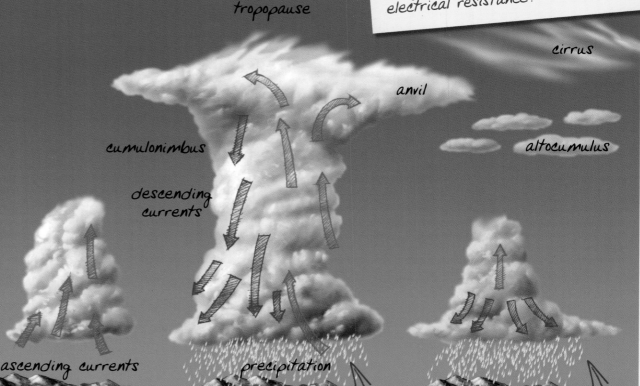

tropopause

cirrus

anvil

cumulonimbus

altocumulus

descending currents

ascending currents

precipitation

Lightning rods
The principle of the lightning rod is: 1. to intercept lightning before it reaches the structure the rod has been set up to protect; 2. to discharge the current into the grou along a thick wire with very low electrical resistance.

Why don't we hear thunder at the same time as we see lightning?
Lightning produces light that travels at 186,410 miles/s, while the speed of the sound of thunder is .2 mile/s (1,100 feet/s). This makes it easy to calculate the distance between the observer and where lightning strikes. We can estimate about a 1/2 mile for each three seconds of difference between the visual perception and the sound.

mature phase
The cumulus has now been transformed into a cumulonimbus. The intense saturation of the air creates a large amount of rain or hail, leading to the most destructive phase of the storm.

dissolution phase
The storm cloud breaks up on the dispersal of the rising air current that nourished it. Strong descending wind currents cause showers of great intensity that end up exhausting the cloud.

Lightning

During the course of a storm the electrical charges that have been generated begin to organize themselves within the clouds so that positive ions are in the upper portion and negative ions are in the lower. The Earth also is charged with positive ions. All of this generates a potential difference of millions of volts, which can produce strong electrical discharges between different points of the same cloud, between different clouds, or even between the clouds and the Earth. The latter electrical discharge is what we call lightning.

Lightning bolts

The lightning bolt is the luminous phenomenon associated with lightning though, this name tends also to be applied to electrical discharges occurring between clouds.

Thunder

The heat produced by the electrical discharge (up to 40,000° F) warms the air, causing it to expand abruptly. Afterwards it contracts on cooling off, creating waves of pressure that are propagated as sound waves. These waves, traveling at the speed of sound (1,100 miles/s), are what we call thunder.

The fireball

This is a rare type of lightning that appears as a luminous ball of about 12 inches in diameter. It moves very quickly from the storm clouds to earth, producing a characteristic whistling sound. It tends to move along power and telephone lines, or to remain suspended in the air. It may explode noisily or disappear in silence.

Types of lightning

These depend on the location of the opposing electrical charges inside and outside the cloud.

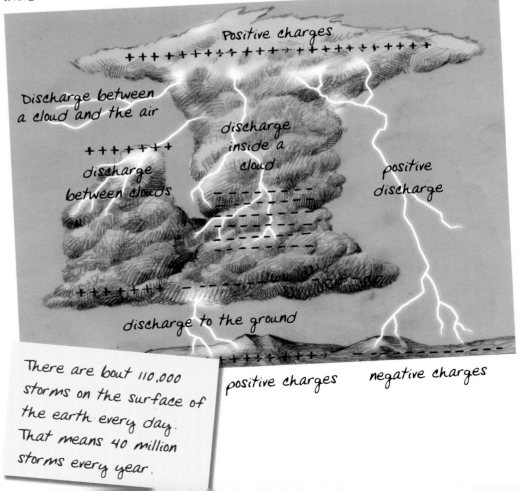

Positive charges

Discharge between a cloud and the air

discharge inside a cloud

discharge between clouds

positive discharge

discharge to the ground

positive charges　　negative charges

There are bout 110,000 storms on the surface of the earth every day. That means 40 million storms every year.

In the Eye of the Hurricane

Cyclones and tornadoes are the most spectacular displays of atmospheric forces. There are few natural phenomena that have such devastating and destructive effects as these whirlwinds, which can cause winds of hundreds of miles per hour, extremely heavy rains and waves more than 16 feet high.

Tornadoes

These are phenomena on a local scale that occur during storms of great intensity. They are characterized by a circular movement in the form of a funnel that descends from the base of a cumuliform cloud, reaching a diameter of hundreds of feet on the surface. They last from a few seconds to several hours and winds can reach over 400 miles per hour.

The waterspout

This is a phenomenon that is similar to a tornado, but it only occurs over the ocean or a lake. It normally lasts about half an hour.

Cyclones

These are enormous masses of air and water vapor that spin at high speed around a low pressure area. They rotate counter-clockwise in the northern hemisphere and clockwise in the southern hemisphere.

A monster in the form of a whirlpool

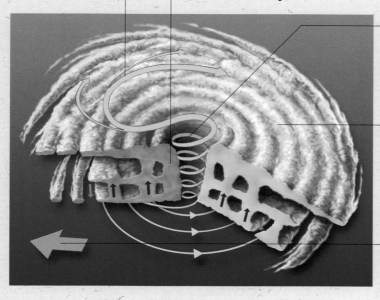

winds | wall of the eye

eye of the cyclone can have a diameter of 18-40 miles

the top of the cyclone can be up to 10 miles high

Cyclones travel from east to west at a speed of about 18 miles per hour.

At the highest levels of the atmosphere the winds turn clockwise, the opposite of what they do at low levels (northern hemisphere).

Mature cyclones range from tens of miles to 125 miles in diameter.

Birth and death of a hurricane

day 1
Cyclones form and intensify over tropical or subtropical disturbances. Winds are a maximum of 28 miles per hour.

day 3
Storms gather around a spiral, forming what are called tropical lows, which turn counter-clockwise.

day 5
Tropical storms form, reaching winds of 38 miles per hour.

day 7
Wind speed is over 70 miles per hour. The hurricane is born.

day 12
On touching land the hurricane begins to lose its strength and disperse as it moves inland.

Hurricanes

This is a type of cyclone that forms over warm tropical waters in the ocean and dies when it hits land. It is an extremely violent storm that moves in a whirling spiral, carrying with it enormous amounts of humidity.

the eye of the hurricane
This is an area of relative calm in the center of a hurricane that extends from sea level to the top of the spiral and is surrounded by a wall of thick clouds heavy with rain. Within the eye, however, due to the high temperature and the presence of warm wind, the evaporated water is rapidly swept upward, leaving dry air that cannot be condensed and is thus without clouds.

different names
In the tropical Atlantic, the Caribbean, and the Pacific Ocean in front of the coasts of Mexico and Central America, this type of cyclone is called a "hurricane." In the Indian Ocean, it is known as a "cyclone." In the western tropical Pacific it is known as a "typhoon," in the Philippines as a "baguio" and in front of the coasts of Australia as a "Willy-Willy."

not all the same
Depending on the intensity of the winds caused by a cyclone, they can be classed as tropical lows (winds up to 38 miles/hour), tropical storms (winds from 38–70 miles/h) or hurricanes (winds over 70 miles/h).

25

At the Weather Station

A visit to a small, traditional weather station would quickly show us how the different meteorological instruments work. By studying and contrasting different measurements, it is easy to learn how to determine what the weather is doing and how to predict what it will be over several days.

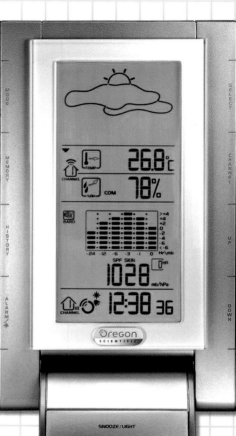

The barometer

This is used to measure air pressure. The metal barometer or aneroid consists of a steel capsule in which a vacuum has been created. When air pressure rises the capsule is compressed, but when pressure goes down the capsule expands. A mechanism translates the movement of the capsule into the movement of a needle on a calibrated scale. The barometer is the basis of all weather forecasts. For meteorological observations it is not just the increase or decrease of pressure that is important, but also the speed with which these changes take place.

The domestic weather station

With interest in the weather high and the cost of electronic devices low, many people today have little weather stations in their own homes that keep them informed about exterior and interior temperatures, relative humidity and atmospheric pressure.

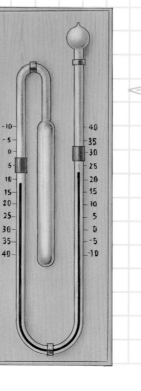

The thermometer

The measurement of air temperature at ground level is taken chiefly with thermometers that contain mercury or alcohol, substances that expand with heat and contract with cold. The measurement of temperature in a specific place is done on different time scales (year, month, day), and the differences between highs and lows describe the variety of thermal conditions.

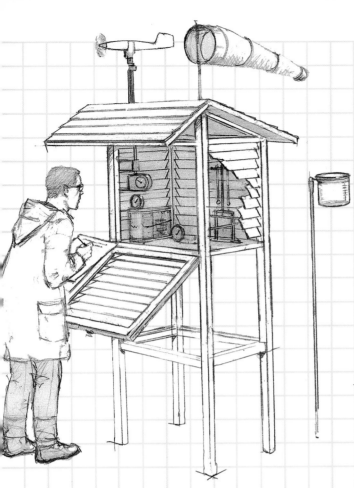

Today everything is automatic

Until recently, observers of the weather had to take data manually from different instruments several times a day. Now autonomous electronic stations register measurements directly onto a computer support system and send them to observation centers by satellite or over the Internet.

The anemometer

This is a device used to measure wind force, or speed. It also is important to know where the wind is coming from. Wind vanes and wind socks are used for this purpose.

The rain gage

This is an instrument that measures the amount of rain that has fallen during a given period of time. It consists of a container with an upper opening of 6 1/2 feet^2 where the water comes in through a funnel to a collector where it is kept. This precipitation is then measured using a probe calibrated in millimeters, which gives us the amount of water that has fallen.

The hygrometer

The hair hygrometer is the most commonly used instrument for measuring the humidity in the air. It is based on the capacity of hair to change length depending on the ambient humidity, so that it shrinks when the environment is dry and gets longer when the air is humid. The hygrometer measures relative humidity, which is the relationship between the amount of water vapor actually in the air (as analyzed) and the amount that there would be if the air were saturated. This measurement is done in percentages.

Will it Rain Tomorrow?

Weather is easy to analyze as it is happening. Making precise forecasts, however, is not so simple. Today meteorologists all over the world are constantly exchanging information collected from 14,000 observation stations on land and at sea, as well as from a dozen satellites. This, in conjunction with computers, allows the the weather to be predicted fairly accurately days in advance.

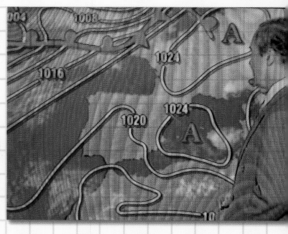

Weather prediction

Weather prediction consists of making projected determinations about the meteorological variables, such as temperature, pressure, humidity, cloudiness, precipitation, etc., that will affect a specific region.

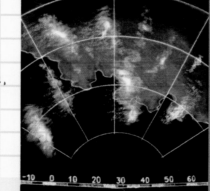

Listening to the weather forecast

All of us at some time have watched the weather report on television or turned on the radio to find out whether we needed to dress warmly or grab an umbrella, or what the weather was going to be like for the weekend, over a vacation, or on a special day.

Radiosonde

This is a device that is carried up into the atmosphere by a balloon inflated with light gas. It is fitted with sensors that determine one or more parameters (pressure, temperature, humidity or wind), and with a transmission system for sending this information to equipment on land. These devices, which have limited duration, can reach an altitude of up to 16 1/2 miles.

Radar meteorology

This is observation instrument that makes it possible to detect the presence of rain at a distance and to estimate its intensity. Consequently these radars are indispensable tools for monitoring and making immediate predictions in cases of intense precipitations in order to minimize damage to people and property.

The satellites

There are two types of artificial satellites, those with a polar orbit that go around the Earth and pass several times over the same point at a specific time; those in geostationary orbit that move around the equator at about 22,370 miles of altitude at the same speed as the spinning of the Earth. This makes them stationary with respect to a specific point.

Meteorological services

These services deal with the processing and storing of information produced in the network of weather stations within each country. They also plan, coordinate, and design meteorological research and prepare forecasts.

Additionally, they are in charge of weather monitoring and serve as links to the meteorological services of other countries. They also coordinate with the Civil Defense service to warn about extreme weather conditions.

A—Summary of the weather forecast for the whole region analyzed

B—Short report of what the weather will be like in the short term

C—Descriptive map of today's weather for the region analyzed

D—High and low temperatures registered the previous day and forecast for today for the major cities, as well as the condition of the sky (C clear, O overcast, P precipitation).

E—Meteorological data, referring to a specific observatory, that are significant for the area where the newspaper is published.

F—Times of the rising and setting of the sun and the moon.

NEWS OF MADRID

Sunday, 30 January, 2005

THE WEATHER

C

IMPROVEMENT IN THE WEATHER
The passage of the depression has brought rain to western Europe and is still producing light snowfalls in the North and East. Temperatures are tending to rise and the sea to calm.

A

B

MONDAY
Sunshine predominates in the western part of Europe with isolated showers in the Mediterranean and snow in the East. Temperatures slightly higher than normal.

TUESDAY
An anticyclone has settled over Europe, which is bringing intense fog to inland valleys. Rain in the Mediterranean and snow in the East are disappearing. Stable temperatures.

MADRID OBSERVATORY

E

MIN. TEMP.:	36° F at 6.12 a.m.
TEMP. MAX.:	46.7° F at 1.45 min
RAIN (24 H):	-
ATM PRES. (7 P.M.):	1.10 HPA
WIND (7 P.M.):	N-3.7 MILES/H
HUMIDITY (7 P.M.):	57%
SKY (7 P.M.):	CLEAR

SUN   MOON

F

SUN		MOON	
SUNRISE TODAY:	8:05 a.m.	MOONRISE TODAY:	11:13 p.m.
SUNSET TODAY:	6:05 p.m.	MOONSET TODAY:	10:34 a.m.
SUNRISE TOMORROW:	8:04 a.m.	MOONRISE TOMORROW:	12:19 a.m.
SUNSET TOMORROW:	6:06 p.m.	MOONSET TOMORROW:	10:44 a.m.

TEMPERATURES (yesterday) / TEMPERATURES (today)

D

EUROPE	min.	max.	sky	min.	max.	sky
Amsterdam	32	35.6	D	35.6	41	C
Athens	33.8	50	P	35.6	51.8	O
Berlín	23	33.8	C	28.4	39.2	C
Copenhagen	26.6	33.8	P	28.4	35.6	O
Lisbon	39.2	50	D	41	51.8	C
London	39.2	46.4	D	39.2	50	C
Madrid	35.6	46.4	D	37.4	50	C
Moscow	10.4	34.8	P	14	24.8	P
París	28.4	37.4	D	32	39.2	C
Rome	35.6	42.8	P	37.4	42.8	O
Vienna	28.4	37.4	P	28.4	39.2	O

WORLD	min.	max.	sky	min.	max.	sky
B. Aires	66.2	91.4	C	68	89.5	O
Chicago	23	35.6	D	17.6	32	C
Cairo	60.8	82.4	C	60.8	86	O
Istanbul	24.8	53.6	P	28.4	53.6	O
Havana	57.2	78.8	C	59	82.4	O
Los Ángeles	44.6	64.4	D	46.4	68	C
Mexicon City	46.4	71.5	D	50	75.2	C
Nairobi	60.8	82.4	C	64.4	86	O
New Delhi	44.6	68	D	46.4	71.5	C
New York	24.8	41	C	28.4	42.8	C
Beijing	39.2	50	C	37.4	46.4	C
Río de Janeiro	71.5	82.4	P	71.5	86	O
Tokyo	42.8	53.6	D	42.8	50	C

What's the Weather?

Meteorology uses a variety of instruments to measure temperature, humidity and pressure in different places and at various altitudes. Weather maps are made from this information. The basic elements of these maps are fronts, low pressure areas (depressions), and anticyclones. With these we can explain which way the clouds are going, where conditions exist for them to produce precipitations, and what direction the winds will take.

Surface maps

These show the lines that join the points that have the same atmospheric pressure. These are called isobars. The lines are drawn at intervals of 4 hPa (hectopascals or millibars).

the depressions

Low pressure areas are indicated on weather maps with an "L." In them, atmospheric pressure decreases toward the center.

anticyclones

These are areas where pressure is higher and on the maps they are represented by an "H." The isobars always indicate an increase of pressure toward the center.

cold fronts and warm fronts

The lines that represent these fronts indicate that the air that is behind the line is colder or warmer than that which is in front of it. Cold fronts are represented in blue by triangles and warm fronts in red by semi-circles.

Good weather

An anticyclonic or high pressure area is generally associated with good weather, since it averts the fronts that move toward it and does not allow ascending movements of air.

Wind and calm

An area where the isobars are very close together indicates strong winds. On the other hand, if these curves are widely separated we are dealing with a calm region.

Which way is the wind going?

The direction of the wind can be deduced by keeping in mind that the wind follows, approximately, the isobars. In an anticyclone in the northern hemisphere the wind moves clockwise and in a low pressure area it goes in the opposite direction. In the southern hemisphere the directions are reversed.

When it rains

Depressions are associated with fronts. The passage of a cold front can mean a drop in temperature and heavy rains, while a warm front can bring a rise in temperature and rains that are light, but continuous.

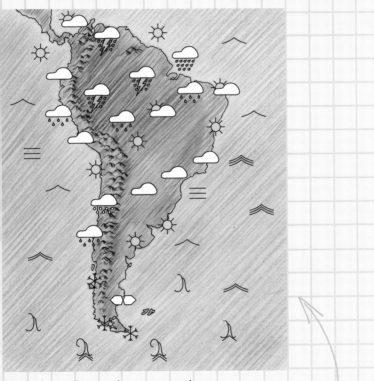

Significant weather charts
These are summaries of surface maps, in which symbols are used to represent the most significant meteorological phenomena that will occur the following day. Normally pictures of a sun, clouds, umbrellas, and ice crystals are used, though these symbols are not internationally regulated.

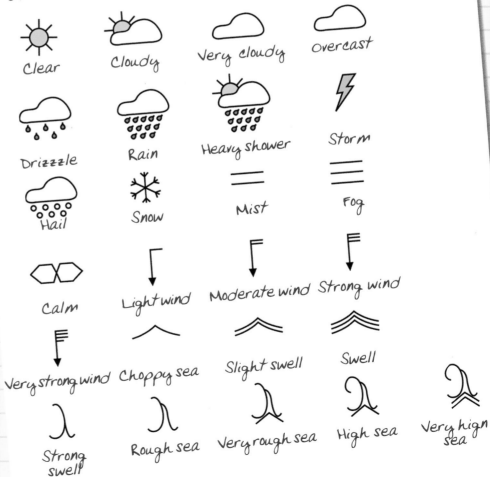

Symbols frequently used on weather maps

Clear

Cloudy

Very cloudy

Overcast

Drizzzle

Rain

Heavy shower

Storm

Hail

Snow

Mist

Fog

Calm

Light wind

Moderate wind

Strong wind

Very strong wind

Choppy sea

Slight swell

Swell

Strong swell

Rough sea

Very rough sea

High sea

Very high sea

Beaufort Scale —Wind Intensity

Grade or force	Denomination	Symbol	Speed		Description of the condition of the sea
			knots	miles/h	
0	Calm		< 1	< 1.2	Like a mirror
1	Light air		1-3	1.2-3.7	Ripples but no foamy crests
2	Light breeze		4-6	4.3-6.8	Wavelets, glassy crests, no breakage
3	Gentle breeze		7-10	7.4-11.8	Wavelets, crests beginning to break, glassy foam, scattered whitecaps
4	Moderate breeze		11-16	12.4-18.6	Longer waves, numerous whitecaps
5	Fresh breeze		17-21	19.2-24.2	Many waves, getting longer, many whitecaps and some spray
6	Strong breeze		22-27	24.8-31	Large waves begin to be formed. Foam crests are seen everywhere. Spray increases and navigation is dangerous for small craft
7	Near gale		28-33	31.6-37.9	Foam is pulled in the direction of the wind. The sea is rough
8	Gale		34-40	38.5-45.9	High, breaking waves. The foam streaks through the air resembling clouds
9	Strong gale		41-47	46.6-54	High waves. Dense streaks of foam. Sea begins to roll and spray reduces visibility
10	Storm		48-55	54.6-63.3	Very high waves with overhanging crests. The surface of the sea looks white. Reduced visibility. The sea rolls.
11	Violent storm		56-63	64-72.7	Exceptionally high waves (vessels with medium tonnage disappear from view). Sea is completely white. Visibility greatly reduced.
12	Hurricane		64-71 >	73.3-82.7 >	The air is filled with foam and spray. Visibility is almost nonexistent

Index

33

What do We Need to Watch the Weather?

By consulting this book and using the equipment presented here you will be able to observe the weather just as a professional meteorologist does and even be able to take a stab at predicting it.

The thermometer makes it possible to know the temperature at the moment, as well as highs and lows over a 24 hour period.

A compass is essential for establishing the precise location of the cardinal points.

The barometer registers atmospheric pressure. When it is high there is usually good weather. When it goes down abruptly, the indication is for bad weather.

An anemometer is necessary to determine the speed of the wind

To find out which direction the wind is coming from you need to observe a weathervane.